Backyard Blooms

A Month by Month Garden Sampler

By Barbara Jones

Backyard Blooms

A Month by Month Garden Sampler

By Barbara Jones

Editor: Deb Rowden
Designer: Kelly Ludwig
Photography: Aaron T. Leimkuehler
Illustration: Eric Sears
Technical Editor: Nan Doljac
Production Assistance: Jo Ann Groves

Published by:
Kansas City Star Books
1729 Grand Blvd.
Kansas City, Missouri, USA 64108

First edition, first printing
ISBN: 978-1-935362-60-9

Printed in the United States of America by
Walsworth Publishing Co., Marceline, MO

Dedication

This book is dedicated to Glenda,
my ever-patient and supportive sister.

Acknowledgements

The book wouldn't have been possible without the great folks at Kansas City Star Publishing and their willingness to fit us into the schedule on short notice. Nor would it have been possible without Henry Glass & Co, my staff and family. A heartfelt thanks to all.

Note

Kits for Backyard Blooms in both fabric lines are available at www.quiltsoup.com while supplies last. QuiltSoup patterns are available at www.quiltsoup.com. For Simply Sweet Fabrics and other QuiltSoup fabric collections, see: www.henryglassfabrics.com.

Contents

The Blocks

Recipe

About the Author

Barbara Jones has been designing quilts since she started making them more than 20 years ago. Her quilts reflect her signature style-whimsical, fun and appliquéd. She now designs the fabrics that make her quilts easily identifiable. Her fabric lines are Bubblegum Basics and Simply Sweet by Henry Glass & Co.

In 2004, she switched careers from molecular biology to start her pattern company, QuiltSoup. The QuiltSoup logo says homemade soups and handmade quilts. She likes both because they come from the heart, and she includes a free recipe in every pattern. QuiltSoup offers kits for quilts made from her fabric.

Barbara lives in Bountiful, Utah, with her husband. You can see more of Barbara's designs, plus find great soup recipes, at www.quiltsoup.com. Select kits for the quilt in this book are also available, while supplies last, at quiltsoup.com.

This is her second Kansas City Star Quilts book. *Cradle to Cradle* was her first.

About this quilt

We had such fun making Backyard Blooms we worked it again in another fabric line called Bubblegum Basics. The coloration is similar. Wouldn't it be fun to see it in a dark colorway or even some larger scale prints that are decidedly modern? The possibilities are endless!

My Backyard Blooms

I love flowers! From the first snow drops in March through the mums of August, I love to see and smell them. My dinner-plate hibiscus bushes bloom about halfway through the season (late July) and the blossoms are larger than both my hands put together. I love to see them and know they are why I plant, feed and sometimes weed! The flowers, birds and fabrics in this quilt all make me happy! Please enjoy making this sampler quilt as much as I did.

General information

A word about **borders:** Due to differences in skills and tools, your quilt center may vary from the ideal measurements by a little bit. We always recommend that you **measure your actual quilt center** before cutting borders to exact lengths. You may cut the border strips at the exact width but leave the piece about 2" longer than called for until you have measured your quilt. Cut to exact lengths after measuring. Measure horizontally through the **center** of your quilt to get the width and vertically to get the length.

General notes regarding appliqué. We prefer needle turn appliqué and used this method to make all the appliqué blocks. In general, the steps are:

1. Overcut the background fabric as instructed. We always ask you to overcut the background by about 1" so you can appliqué the block, press and trim down to the actual size you need. Because the backgrounds are overcut, patches must be kept at least 3/4" in from the outside edges of the background fabric to allow for trimming. The only exceptions are when we want you to catch the edge of a patch (e.g. the bottom of a pot or basket) in the seam allowance. In that case, we have taken the overcut into account and allowed for it in your templates. You simply line up the bottom of your patch (with the seam allowance included) with the edge of the background fabric.

2. Prepare templates from template plastic or freezer paper for each patch by tracing the shapes found in the pattern sheets. Cut these templates out on the line.

3. Place templates over right side of fabric and trace around each lightly with pencil. Cut patches from fabric and add 1/4" seam allowance by eyes as you cut. This is a little large but I like to work with a clean cut when I appliqué to reduce fraying. I trim the seam allowance to a scant 3/16" as I stitch each patch. If you find this redundant, just add a scant 3/16" seam allowance as you cut each patch out.

4. Place patches on background fabric and glue baste in place. I prefer Roxanne's Glue-Baste-It or Appli-glue by Jillily Studios. Roxanne's may be found at quilt shops and Appli-glue may be found at www.jillillystudio.com.

5. Appliqué each patch with 100% cotton thread that matches the patch, not the background.

6. If you can't find an exact match and have to choose between a shade lighter and a shade darker, choose the darker. We find darker is less visible.

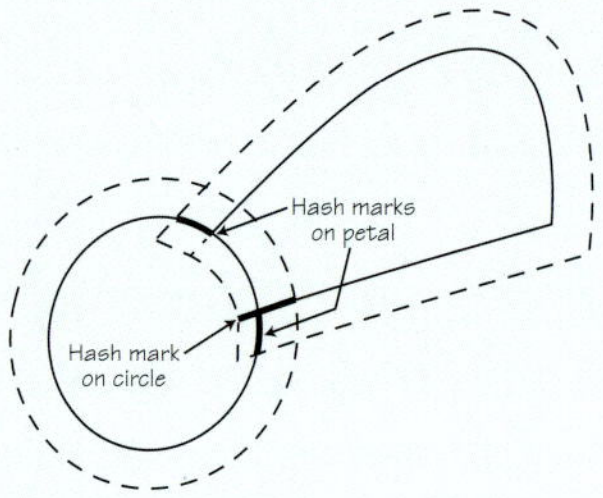

To help accurately position needle-turn appliqué patches that over and under lap, mark a hash mark in the seam allowance of both patches where they meet. These marks will be turned under when you appliqué and no one will be any the wiser!

Other Stuff

1. Cutting: For best use of fabric, cut the largest pieces first. Leftover fabric may be used to piece the backing.

2. Seam allowance is 1/4" and is abbreviated as s.a.

3. Finished measurements are **not** the cut measurements. Finished measurements are the size the block or quilt measures once it has been sewn together.

Simply Sweet Color Swatches & Fabric requirements

Pink Vine
3/8 yard

Red Dot
1 1/3 yard

Red Check
3/8 yard

Green Vine
1/2 yard

Green Dot
1/3 yard

Green Oval
1/4 yard

Yellow Oval
1/3 yard

Yellow Pencil Stripe
1/2 yard

Blue Vine
1/4 yard

Blue Check
1/8 yard

Blue Pencil Stripe
1/2 yard

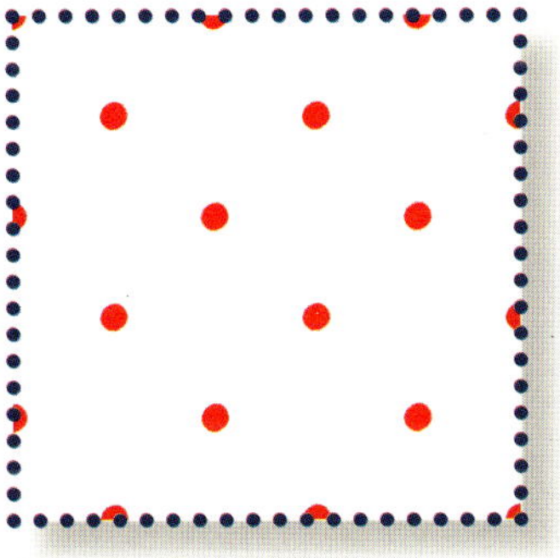

White with Red
Pindots 1 yard

White Floral
2 1/4 yards
Note: this is generous so border strips can be cut from length. We used the remainder on the back.

Binding	5/8 yard
Batting	2 yards
Backing	3 2/3 yards

Super Saver Pre-Cutting Instructions

A word about cutting: It is important for you to cut as directed in order to get the best use of your fabric.

A word about scraps: Save your scraps! A scrap to me is anything that is bigger than 1 1/2" square! We suggest a little scrap bin (old shoebox? plastic bag?) to keep these smaller pieces organized for easy use throughout the project.

A little pre-cutting is needed to get the best use of your fabric. You also want to keep these cuts organized. We recommend you gather 6 Ziploc bags and label them Blocks 1-6. These are for cuts you will make. We also want you to **save all your scraps.** We recommend plastic bags or bins for these scraps. We usually sort these scraps by colors...you know...all the pinks together, all the reds, blues, greens and yellows together as well. You can use them for small appliqué or pieced patches. Pre-cutting is listed by color.

We have included fabric descriptions and color swatches on page 7 for easy reference. Please pre-cut in the order we give. Then bag it and tag it and you are good to go!

Note: wof means width of fabric.

Pink Vine
No pre-cutting required.

Red Dot
Cut 1- 14 1/2" x wof strip and set aside for block 6.
Cut 1 - 16 1/2" square and set aside for block 2.
From remainder, cut 1 - 4" x 14" strip and set aside for block 6.
Remaining piece is used as called for in block patterns.

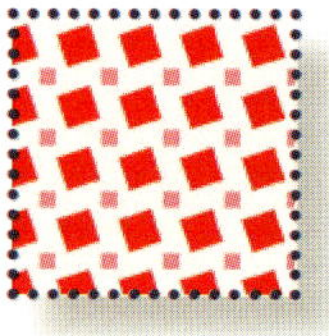

Red Check
Cut 1 - 3 1/2" x wof strip. Set aside for blocks 2 and 6.
Remainder is used as called for in block patterns.

Green Vine
Cut 2 - 3 1/2" x wof strip and set aside for blocks 4, 5 and 6.
Remainder is used as called for in block patterns.

Green Dot
No pre-cutting required.

Green Oval
No pre-cutting required.

Yellow Oval
No pre-cutting is required when blocks are worked in order.

Yellow Pencil Stripe
No pre-cutting is required when blocks are worked in order.

Blue Vine
Cut 1 - 2" x wof strip and set aside for block 3.
Remainder is used as called for in block patterns.

Blue Check
No pre-cutting required.

Blue Pencil Stripe
Cut 1 - 16 1/2" square for block 4 and set aside.
Cut 2 - 3 1/2" x remaining width of fabric and set aside for block 6.

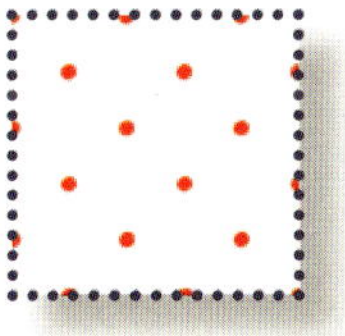

White with Red Pindots
Cut 6 - 2" x wof strips and set aside for inner borders.
Cut 4 - 1 1/2" x wof strips and set aside for block 1.
Cut 1 - 16 1/2" square and set aside for block 3.
Remainder is used as called for in block patterns.

White Floral
Cut 1 - 9" x 21" from one end of fabric. Set aside for blocks 4 and 6.
Cut 2 - 5" x **length** of fabric strips and set aside for top and bottom outer borders.
Cut 2 - 4 1/2" x **length** of fabric strips and set aside for side outer borders.
Remainder is used as called for in block patterns.

Note: We also used leftovers on the back of our quilt.

Backyard Blooms

59" x 69 3/4"

Month 1

Trowel Block

18" x 12" finished

Make 1

Appliqué templates are on pages 20-21.

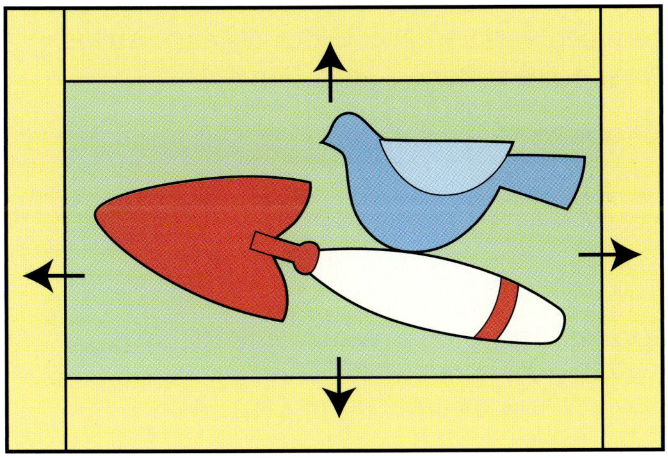

Trowel Block Cutting

Green Vine	Cut 1 - 16 1/2" x 9 1/2" block background. Block is trimmed to 15 1/2" wide x 8 1/2" high after appliqué and pressing.
Yellow Oval	Cut 2 - 2 1/2" x 15 1/2" for top and bottom of trowel block. Cut 2 - 2" x 12 1/2" for sides of trowel block.
White Floral	Cut 1 trowel handle.
Red Dot	Cut 1 trowel head, 1 trowel "tang", and 1 stripe for handle.
Blue Vine	Cut 1 bird facing left.
Blue Check	Cut 1 bird wing, also facing left.

Trowel Block Assembly

1. Prepare and position patches as shown on pattern.
   Note: Appliqué stripe onto handle before stitching the handle to the background. Appliqué, press and trim to 15 1/2" x 8 1/2".

2. Sew Yellow Oval 2 1/2" x 15 1/2" strips to top and bottom of trowel block. Press to yellow.

3. Sew Yellow Oval 2" x 12 1/2" strips to both sides of block and press to yellow.

Month 1

Nine-Patch Sashes

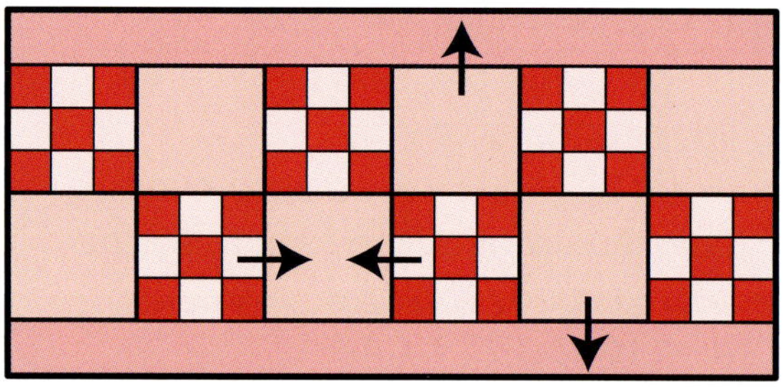

9" x 18" finished

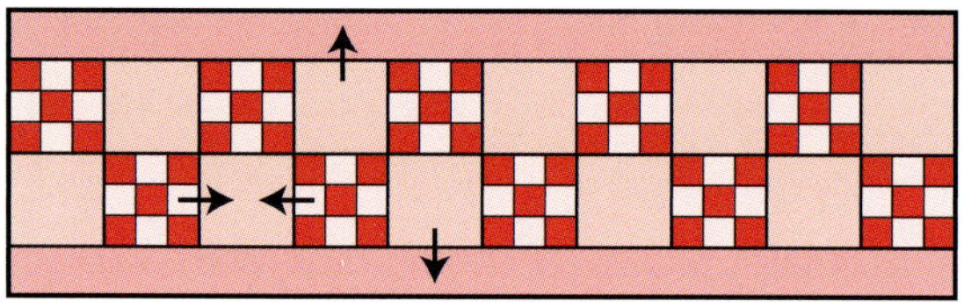

9" x 30" finished

Both are worked at the same time. Cutting and assembly is for both.

Nine Patch Sashes - Cutting

Red Check: Cut 2 - 3 1/2" x width of fabric strips. From these cut 16 - 3 1/2" squares for alternate blocks in nine patch sashes.

White with Red Pindot: Cut 4 - 1 1/2" x width of fabric strips for nine patch blocks.

Red Dot: Cut 5 - 1 1/2" x width of fabric strips for nine patch blocks.

Pink Vine: Cut 3 - 2" x width of fabric strips. From these cut 2 - 2" x 30 1/2" strips and 2 - 2" x 18 1/2" strips.

Nine Patch Sashes - Assembly

Nine patches are made with strip sets.
Sew one white 1 1/2" x width of fabric strip between 2 red 1 1/2" x width of fabric strips. Press to red. Make 2 sets. (Fig A).

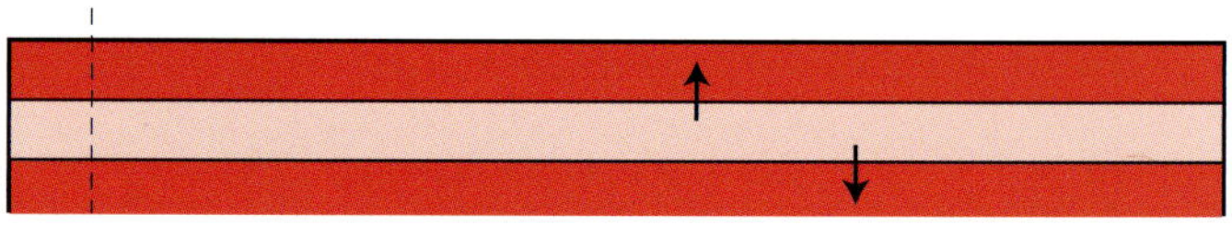

Fig A

Sew one red 1 1/2" x width of fabric strip between 2 white 1 1/2" x width of fabric strips. Press to red. Make 1 set (Fig B).

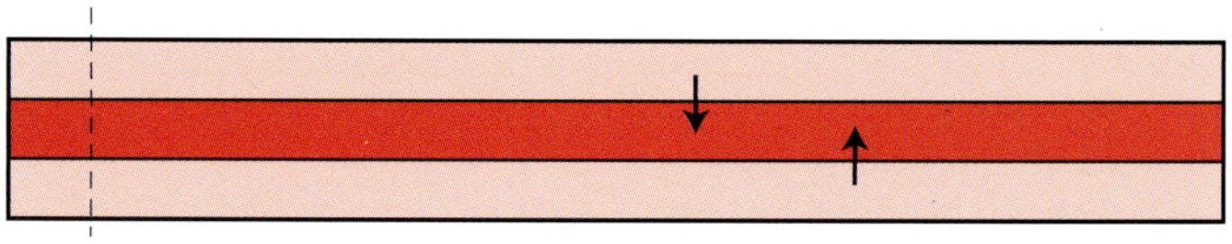

Fig B

Cut 1 1/2" segments across the strip sets as shown by dashed line. Cut 32 segments from A and 16 from B.

Sew the segments into nine patches as shown (Fig C). Make 16 nine patch blocks. Blocks now measure 3 1/2" square and finish at 3".

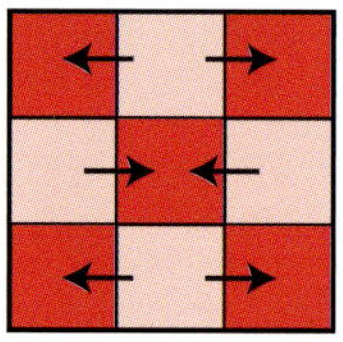

Fig C

Sew the nine patches to red check 3 1/2" alternate blocks as shown. Make 1 short and 1 long sash. Press to alternate blocks. Sew 2" x 18 1/2" pink strips to the top and bottom of the short sash and press to pink.

Sew 2" x 30 1/2" pink strips to top and bottom of long sash and press to pink.

Set these sashes aside for now.

Month 2

Heart Flower Block

15" x 18" finished

Make 1

Appliqué templates are on page 22.

Cutting

Red Dot	Overcut 1 - 16 1/2" square for heart block background. Block is trimmed to 15 1/2" square after appliqué and pressing.
Red Check	Cut 1 - 3 1/2" x 15 1/2" strip for top of heart block.
Pink Vine	Cut 4 - large hearts.
White with Red Pindot	Cut 4 - small hearts.
Green Vine	Cut 4 - leaves.
White Floral	Cut 1 - flower center.

Assembly

1. To position the patches as shown, it is helpful to finger press a few creases in your background block. First, fold the background in half (with right sides out) and lightly crease the fold line. Repeat this horizontally and on both diagonals. You will be able to see where the center of the block is and can place patches easily (Fig D).

Fig D

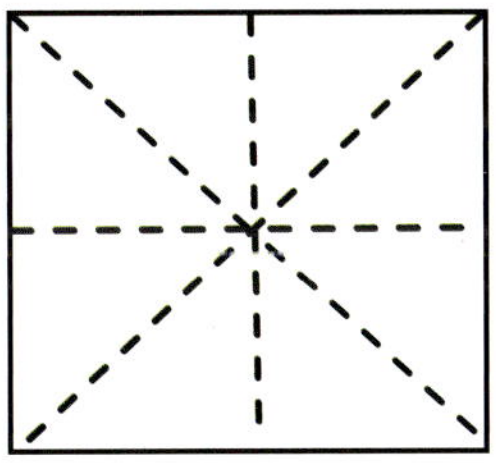

2. Glue baste in place and appliqué. I chose to cut away from behind the hearts so the red did not shadow through. This is optional and a matter of personal preference. If you chose to do this, be careful not to cut through the front of your work. Eeeeeeek!

3. Press. Trim block to 15 1/2" square.

4. Sew red stripe 3 1/2" x 15 1/2" strip to the top of heart block and press to stripe.

Month 3

Hibiscus Pot Block

18" x 21" finished

Make 1

Appliqué templates are on pages 23-26.

Blue Check Cut 1 - 3 1/2" x 9" for middle of pot.

Blue Vine Cut 1 - 2" x 10 1/2" for top pot band.

Cut 1 - 2" x 9" for bottom of pot.

Yellow Oval Cut 1 - 3 1/2" x 21 1/2" strip for side of hibiscus block.

Yellow Pencil Stripe Cut 1 leaf 6.

Green Dot Cut 1 left stem, 1 right stem.

Cut 1 leaf 2, leaf 5, leaf 7.

Green Oval Cut 1 leaf 3, leaf 4.

Green Vine Cut 1 leaf 1.

Pink Vine Cut 1 hibiscus petals 1, 2, 3, 4.

Red Dot Cut 1 flower center.

Cutting

White with Red Pindot

Overcut 1 - 16 1/2" square for appliqué portion of the block.

Cut 2 - 2" x 3" rectangles for sides of pot band.

Cut 1 and 1 reverse Template B by first folding fabric in half, right sides out. Position template on fabric and cut directly around it with rotary cutter. Be careful not to cut your fingers! If this makes you too nervous, trace around the template with a pencil and then cut away the traced line using rotary cutter and ruler or scissors.

Assembly

Appliqué the Hibiscus

Place the patches onto the background in the usual manner. Position the left stem so the bottom of it will be caught in the seam allowance once the block has been trimmed and sewn to the pot. Appliqué. Press and trim to 15 1/2" square.

Make the Pot

Unit is 6 1/2" x 15 1/2".

The pot requires 2 templates, "A" which is the pot and "B" which are the pieces that are sewn to the sides of the pot. Prepare one of each and note the seam line on template A.

Sew blue check 3 1/2" x 9" to blue vine 2" x 9" pot bottom. Press to blue vine. Align the seam line on the pot with the seam line on template A.

--continued on next page

(continued from previous page)
Cut directly around the template using a rotary cutter. If this makes you too nervous, trace the pot and then cut out with scissors. The idea is to piece and then cut the pot from the pieced strips.

Sew white with red pindot "B" patches to both sides of pot. Press to white.

Sew white 2" x 3" to both ends of blue pot band and press to white. Sew this to the pot bottom.

Assemble the Block

Sew hibiscus to pot and press seam to pot. Sew 3 1/2" x 21 1/2" yellow oval to right hand side of block. Press to the yellow oval.

Month 4

Cabbage Roses Block

15" x 18" finished

Make 1 - *Appliqué templates are on pages 27-29.*

Cutting

Blue Pencil Stripe

Overcut 1- 16 1/2" square for block background. This is trimmed to 15 1/2" square after appliqué and pressing.

White Floral	Cut 1 small and 2 large outer roses.
Yellow Oval	Cut 2 middle roses.
Yellow Stripe	Cut 1 middle rose.
Red Dot	Cut 3 rose centers.
Green Dot	Cut 1 leaf 1, leaf 4.
Green Oval	Cut 1 leaf 2, 3.
Green Vine	Cut 1 - 3 1/2" x 15 1/2" strip for bottom of block.

Assembly

1. Position the appliqué patches as shown on the pattern. Appliqué, press. I chose to cut away behind the cabbage roses so the background wouldn't shadow through. This is optional and is a personal preference. Trim the block to 15 1/2" square.

2. Sew green vine 3 1/2" x 15 1/2" strip to the bottom of the block. Press to green.

Month 5

Gardener's Hat Block

30" x 15" finished

Make 1

Appliqué templates are on pages 30-34.

Cutting

Yellow Pencil Stripe	Overcut 1 - 16 1/2" x 28 1/2" rectangle for hat block background.
Green Vine	Cut 1 - 3 1/2" x 15 1/2" for left side of block.
Red Dot	Cut 1 hat brim, 1 flower center for hat and 1 circle for upright flower.
Red Check	Cut 1 hat.
White Floral	Cut 1 hat band, bow, left and right bow ties.
Pink Vine	Cut 1 flower head for upright flower, 1 flower for hat.
Green Dot	Cut 1 stem, 1 left leaf for upright flower.
Green Oval	Cut 1 right leaf for upright flower and 2 leaves for hat.
Blue Vine	Cut 2 birds, 1 facing left and 1 facing right.
Blue Check	Cut 2 bird wings, 1 facing left and 1 facing right.

Assembly

1. Position patches as shown. The hat bow is marked and cut as a single piece to make placement easier. The center of the bow is covered by the hat flower. Cut the 2 loops apart as indicated on your pattern after you have placed them on the block and before you stitch them. Appliqué, press and trim to 27 1/2" x 15 1/2".

2. Sew green vine 3 1/2" x 15 1/2" to left hand side of block. Press to green.

Month 6

Basket Panel Block

15 3/4" x 48" finished

Make 1

Appliqué templates are on pages 35-39.

Cutting

Red Dot Cut 1 - 14 1/4 x width of fabric strip. This is an overcut and is trimmed to 13 1/4" x 42 1/2" after appliqué and pressing.

Cut 1 - 3 1/2" x 13 1/4" for right end of panel.

Red Check Cut 1 - 3 1/2" x 13 1/4" for right end of panel.

Green Dot Cut 1 stem facing left and 1 facing right.

Cut 2 double leaves, cut 2 vine leaves, 1 each for right and left vines.

Cut 1 stem for center flower.

Green Oval Cut 1 vine leaf for left stem.

Cut 1 left leaf for center flower.

Green Vine Cut 1 - 3 1/2" x 15 1/2" strip for bottom of block, left hand side.

Cut 1 right leaf for center flower.

Cut 2 vine leaves, 1 each for right and left vines.

Yellow Oval Cut 1 center flower.

Yellow Pencil Stripe Cut 2 vine flowers.

Pink Vine Cut 1 circle for center flower and 2 circles for vine flowers.

Blue Pencil Stripe

Cut 2 - 3 1/2" x wof from leftover rectangle. Sew end to end into one continuous strip. Press seam open. From this cut 1 - 3 1/2" x 33 1/2" strip for bottom of block, right hand side.

Cut 1 bird facing right.

Blue Vine Cut 1 vine leaf for right stem.

Blue Check Cut 1 bird wing, facing right.

White Floral Cut 1 basket and 1 handle.

Assembly

1. Position patches as shown in pattern and appliqué. Press and trim to 13 1/4" x 42 1/2".

2. Sew red check and red dot 3 1/2" x 13 1/4" strips together, then sew to right end of panel. Sew with red check located between the 2 pieces of red dot. Press both seams to check.

3. Sew green vine 3 1/2" x 15 1/2" strip to blue strip 3 1/2" x 33 1/2" strip and press to blue. Sew this strip to bottom of basket panel. Press to the strip.

Quilt Assembly

The quilt center is assembled in 3 sections: left, right and bottom. Sections are sewn together, then borders are added. Please see General Information on page 5 for reminders about cutting borders to length.

Left

Assembly - Left Section

1. Sew heart flower block and cabbage rose block together. Orient the blocks so the 3 1/2" strip on the heart flower block is up and the strip on the cabbage rose block is down. Press to heart flower block.

2. Sew nine patch long sash to bottom of gardener's hat block. Press to nine patch sash.

3. Sew gardener's hat section to the bottom of the heart flower/cabbage rose blocks.

Right

Assembly - Right Section

1. Sew nine patch short sash (9 1/2" x 18 1/2") to bottom of trowel block.

2. Sew hibiscus block to bottom of nine-patch sash that is below the trowel block. Press to the nine patch.

Assembly - Sew Sections Together

1. Sew left section to right section to make upper section. Press open.

2. Sew basket panel to bottom of upper section. Press to basket panel

Quilt Borders

Borders - Cutting

White with Red Pindot

Cut 6 - 2" x width of fabric strips. Remove selvage ends. Sew end to end into one continuous strip. From this cut as follows:

Cut 2 - 2" x 58 1/2" strips for side borders.

Cut 2 - 2" x 51 1/2" strips for top and bottom borders.

White Floral Cut 2 - 4 1/2" x 61 1/4" strips for side borders.

Cut 2 - 5" x 59 1/2" strips for top and bottom borders. These are wider than the side borders.

Borders - Assembly

1. Sew white 2" x 58 1/2" strips to sides of quilt. Press to white.
2. Sew white 2" x 51 1/2" strips to top and bottom of quilt. Press to white.
3. Sew white floral 4 1/2" x 61 1/4" strips to sides of quilt. Press to white floral.
4. Sew white floral 5" x 51 1/2" strips to top and bottom of quilt. Press to white floral.

Trowel Block

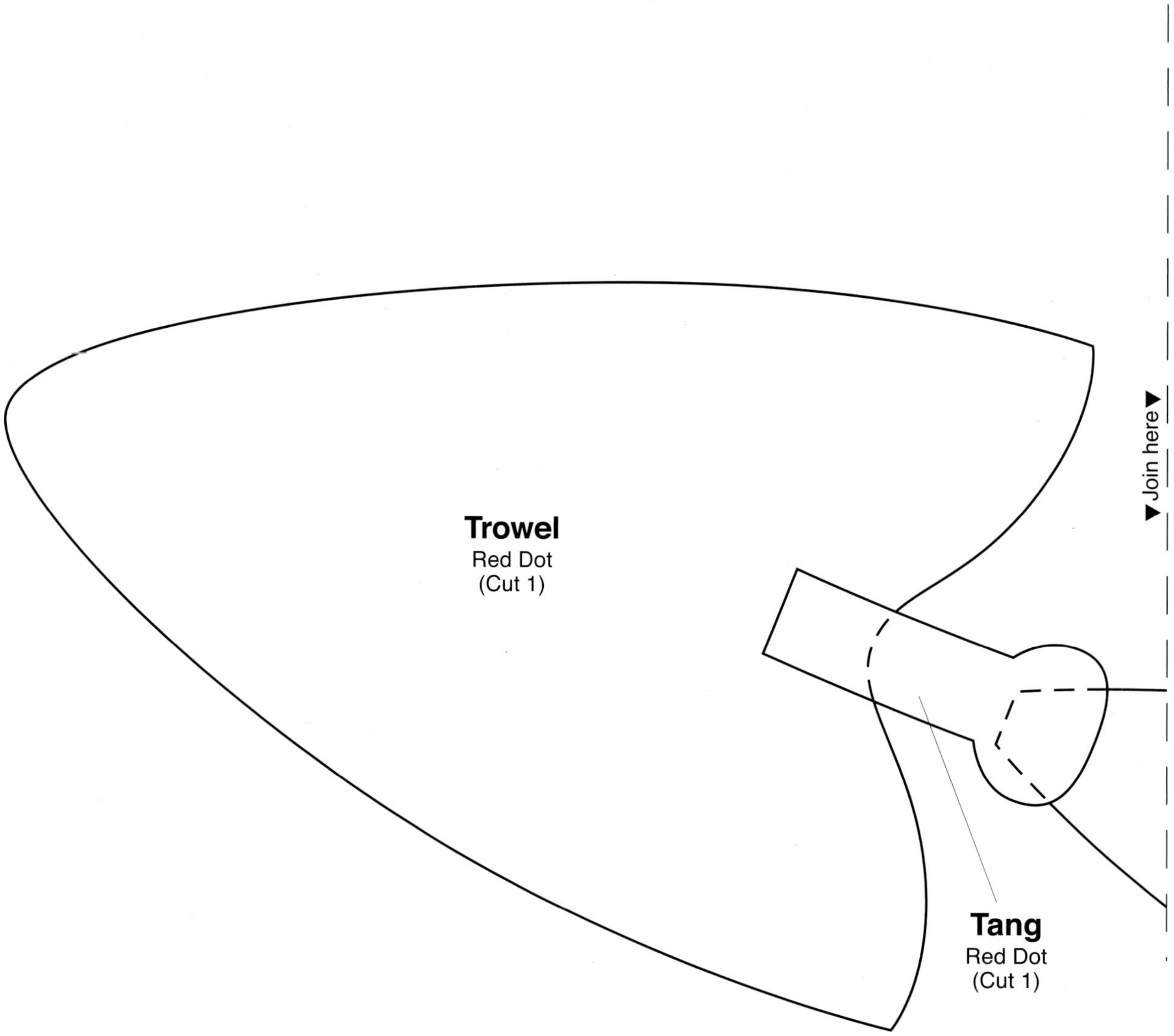

Trowel Block

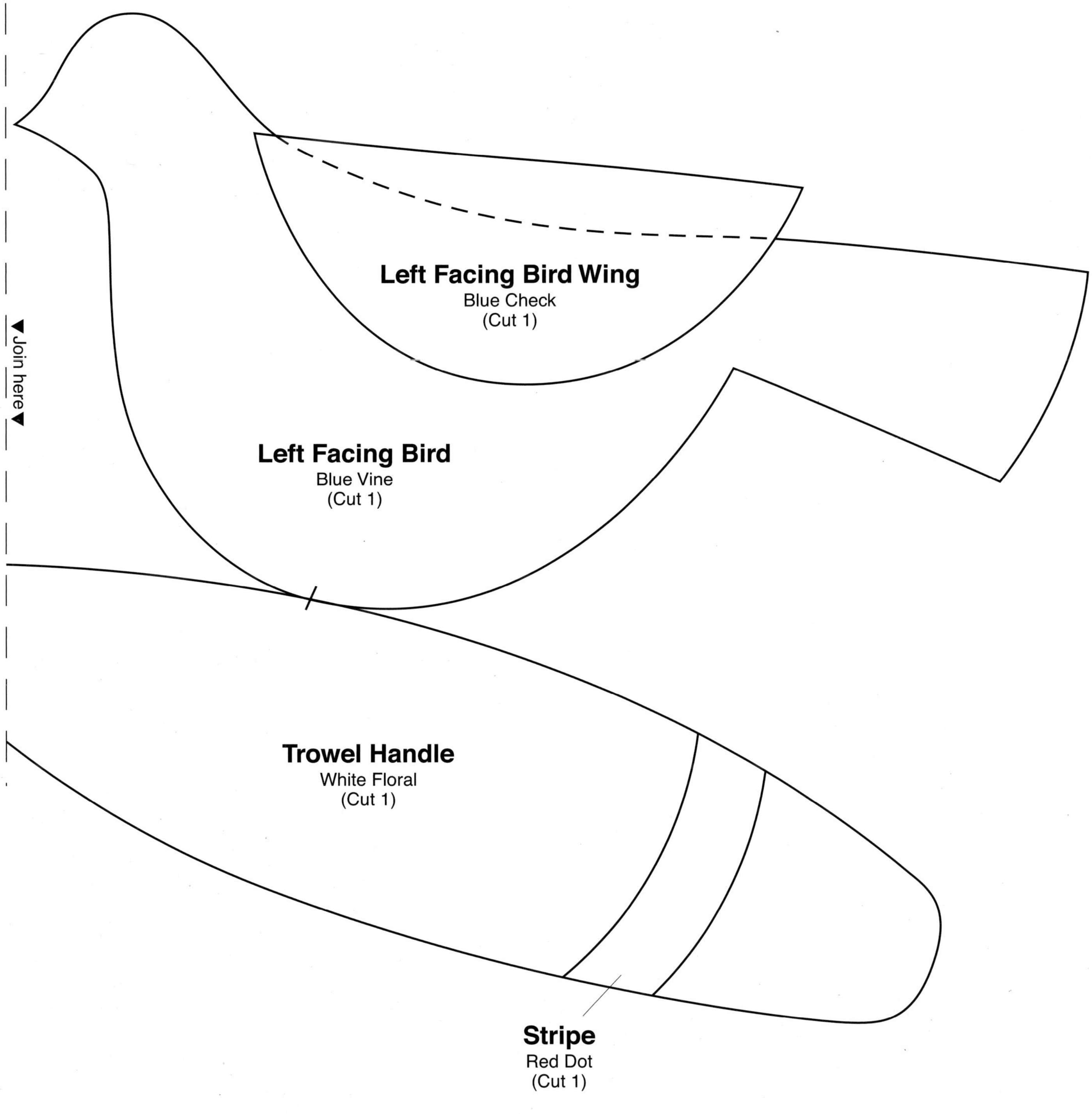

Heart Block

Leaf
Green Vine
(Cut 4)
Large Heart
Pink Vine
(Cut 4)
Small Heart
White with Red Pindot
(Cut 4)
Center
Circle or Flower
White Floral
(Cut 1)
Finger crease center lines in all directions

Hibiscus Block

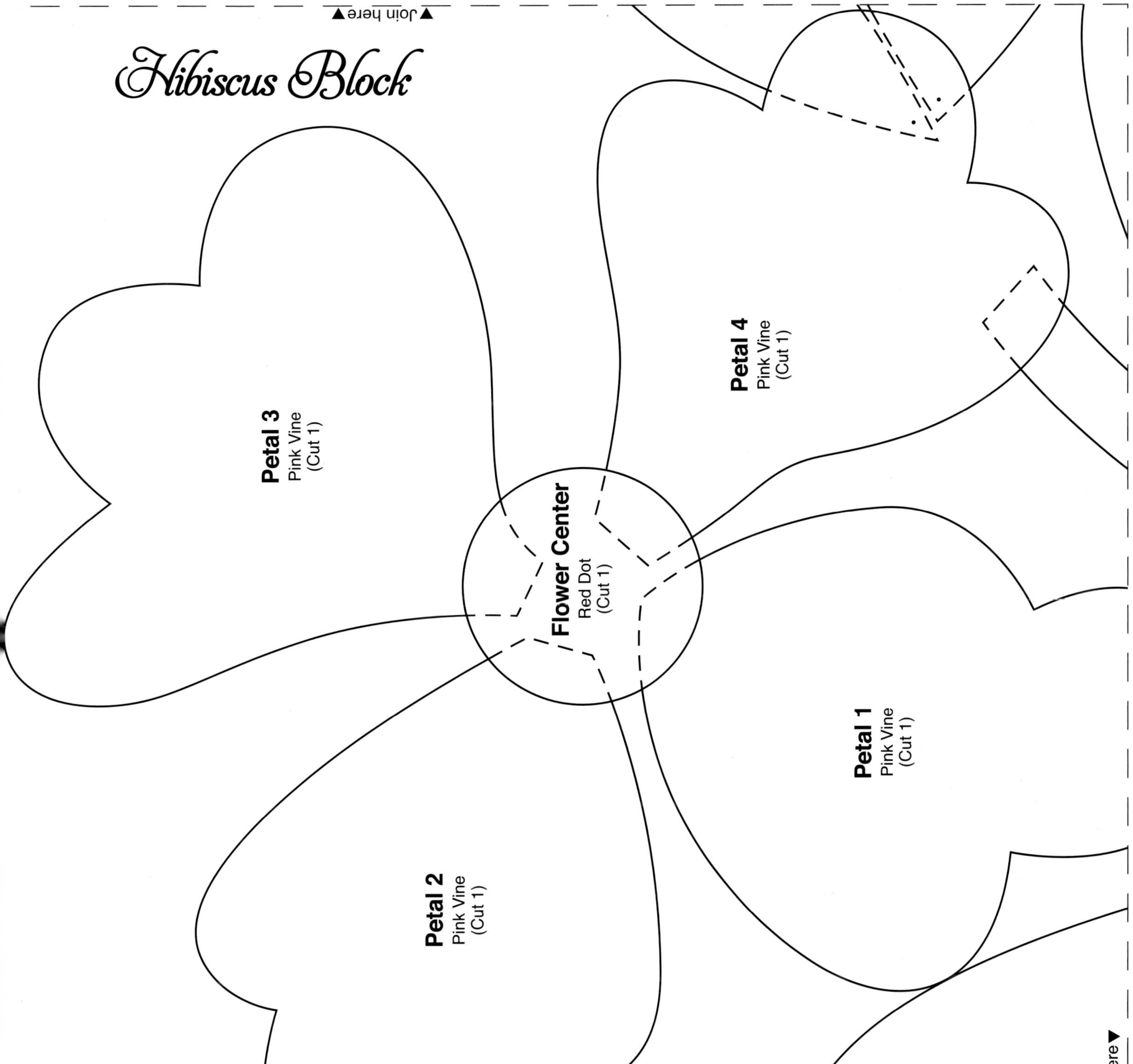

Hibiscus Block, cont.

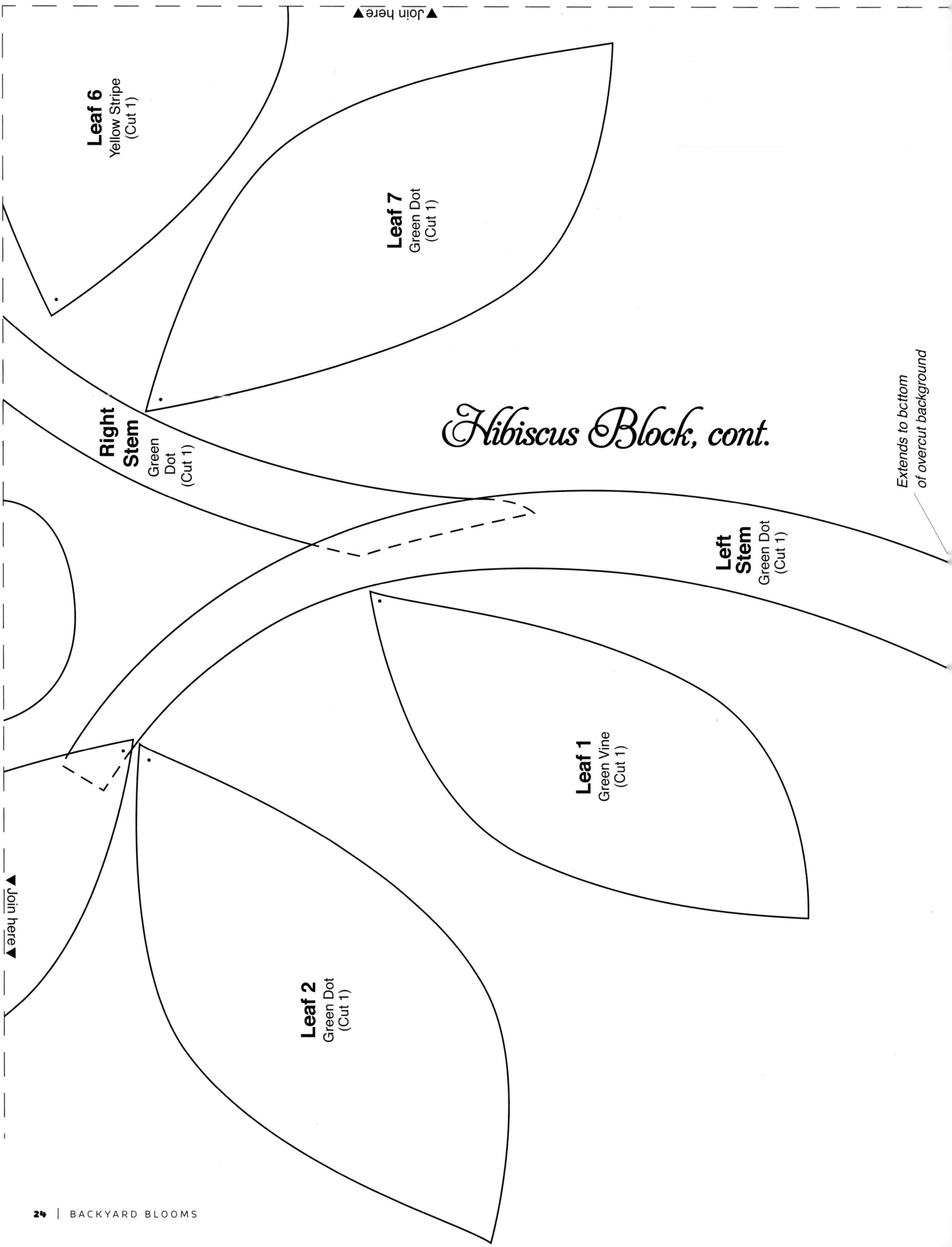

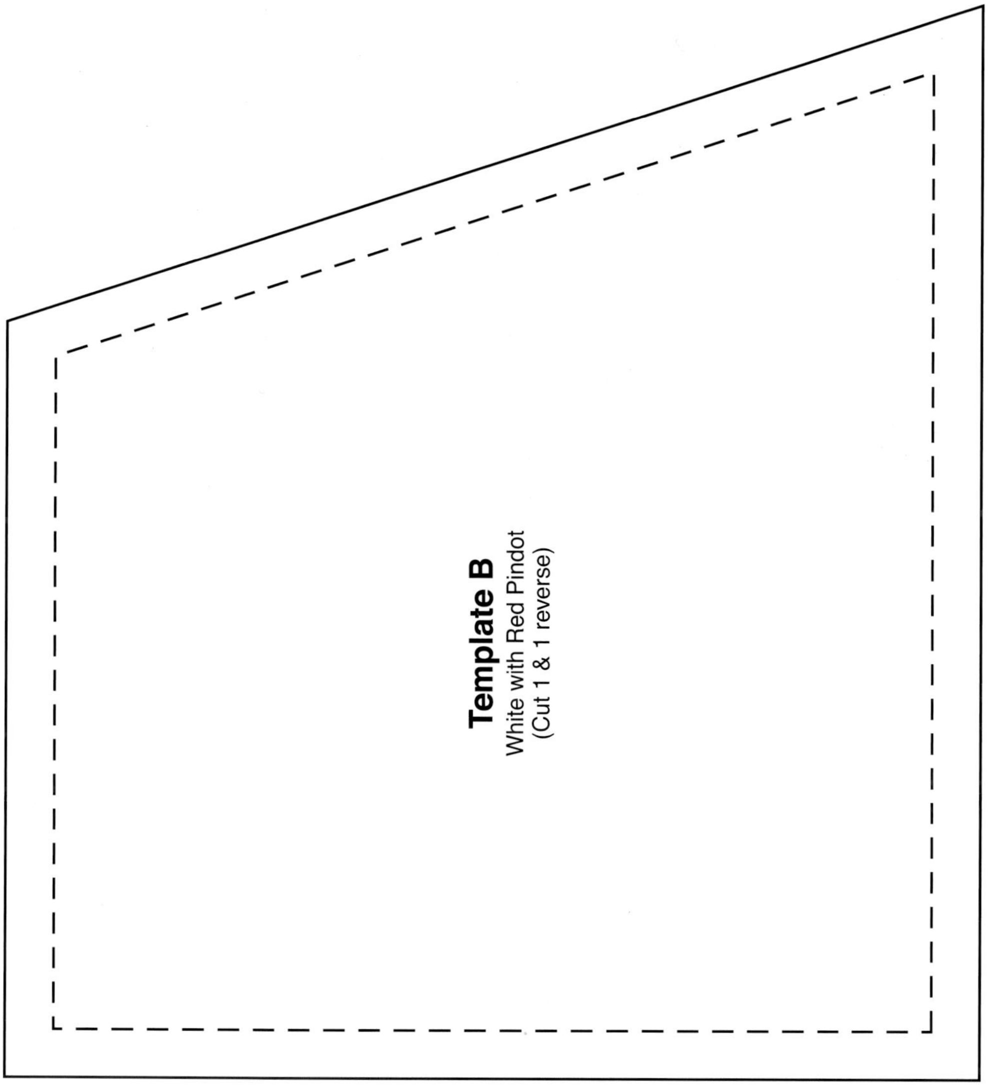

Hibiscus Block, cont.

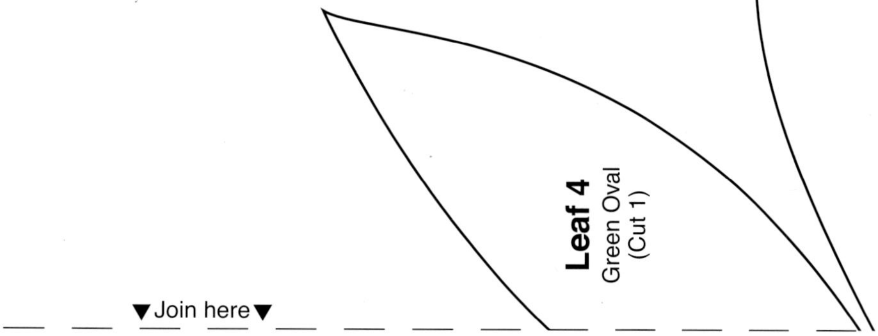

Hibiscus Block, cont.

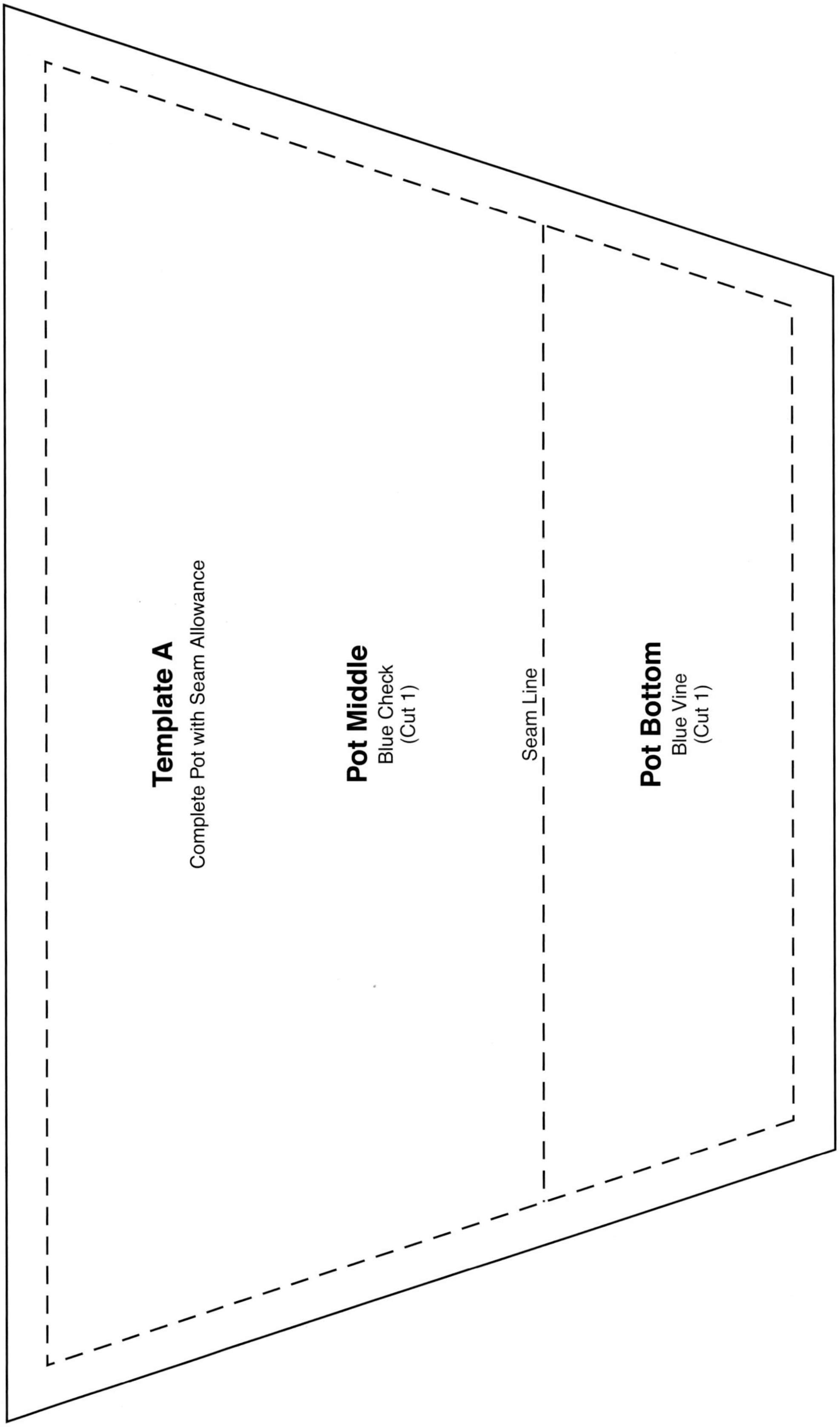

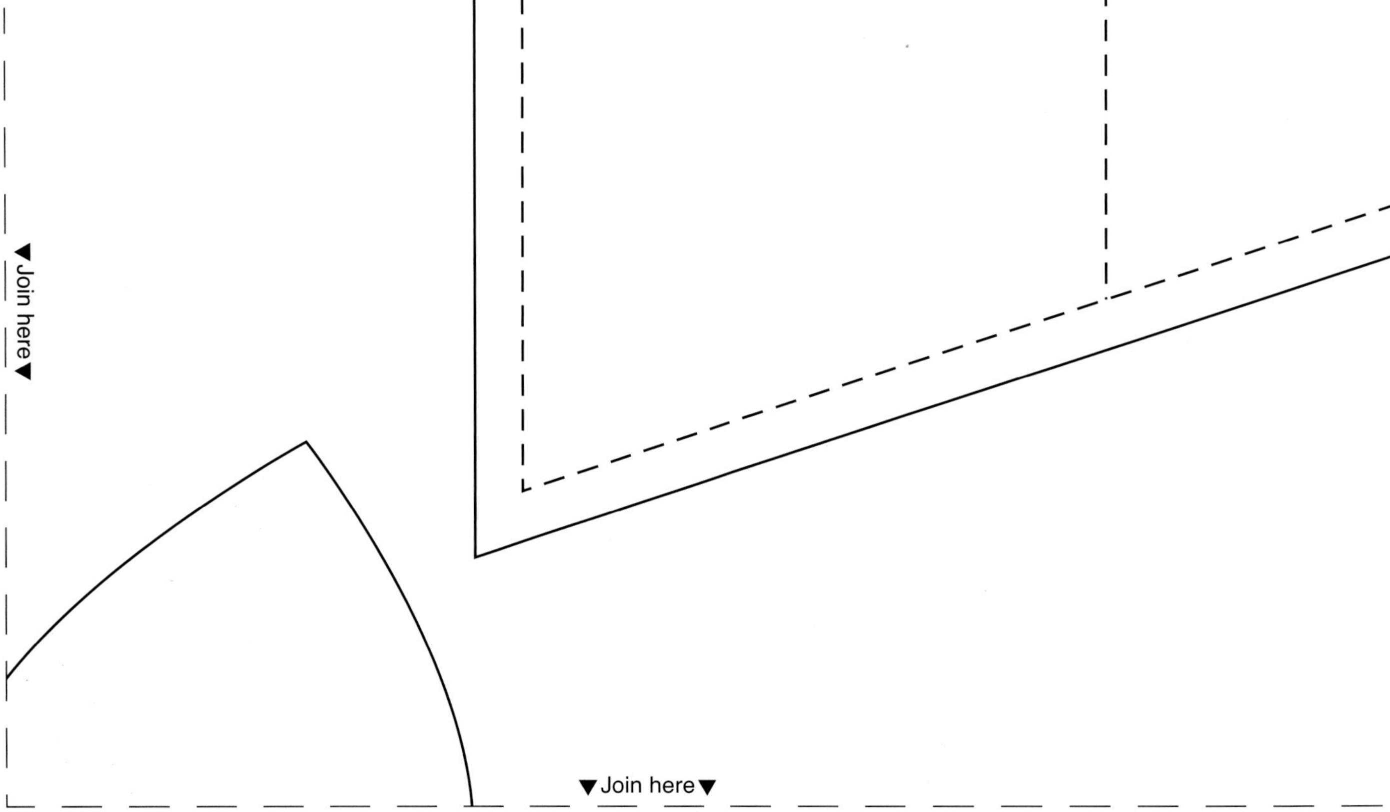

Cabbage Roses Block

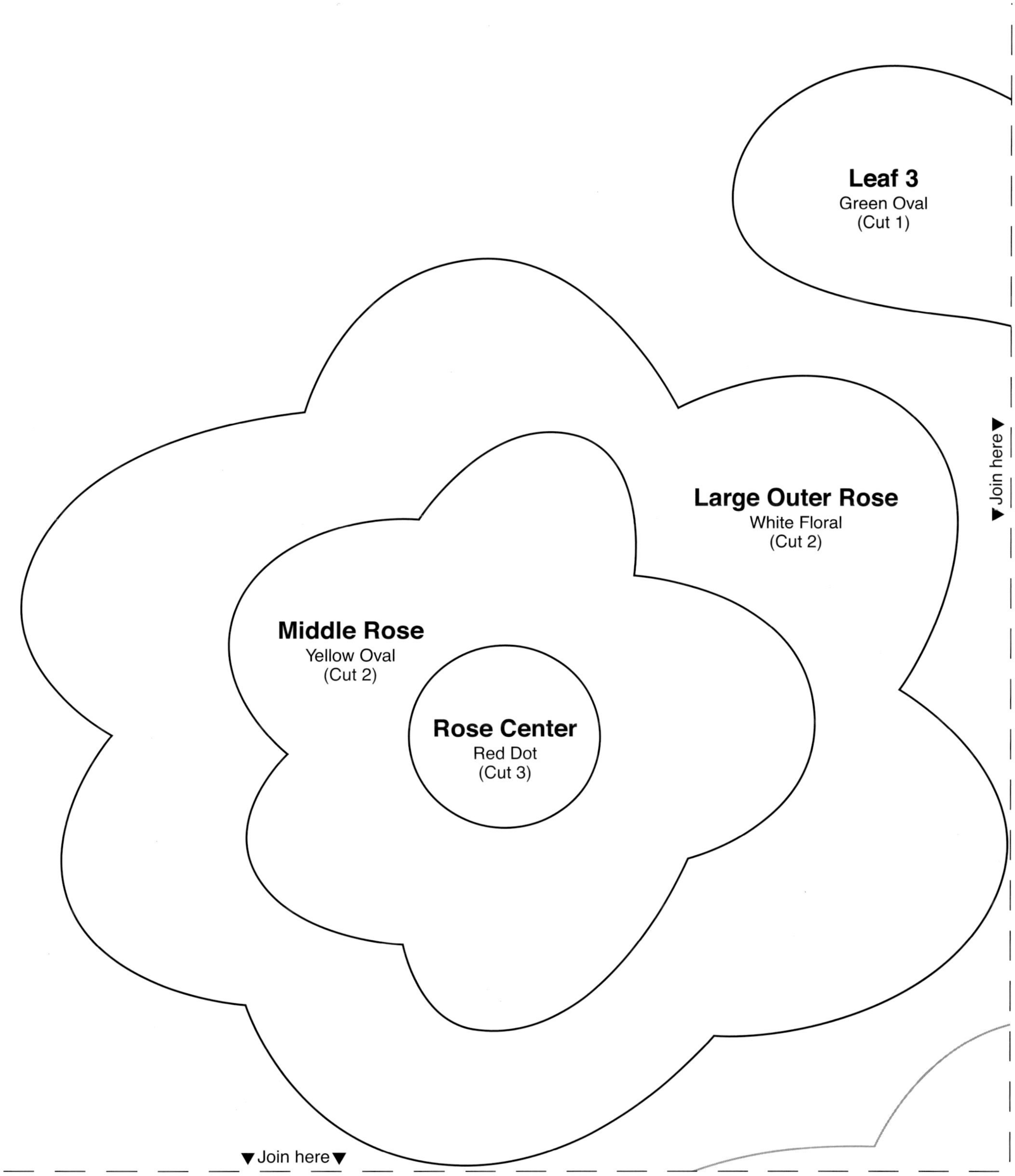

Cabbage Roses Block, cont.

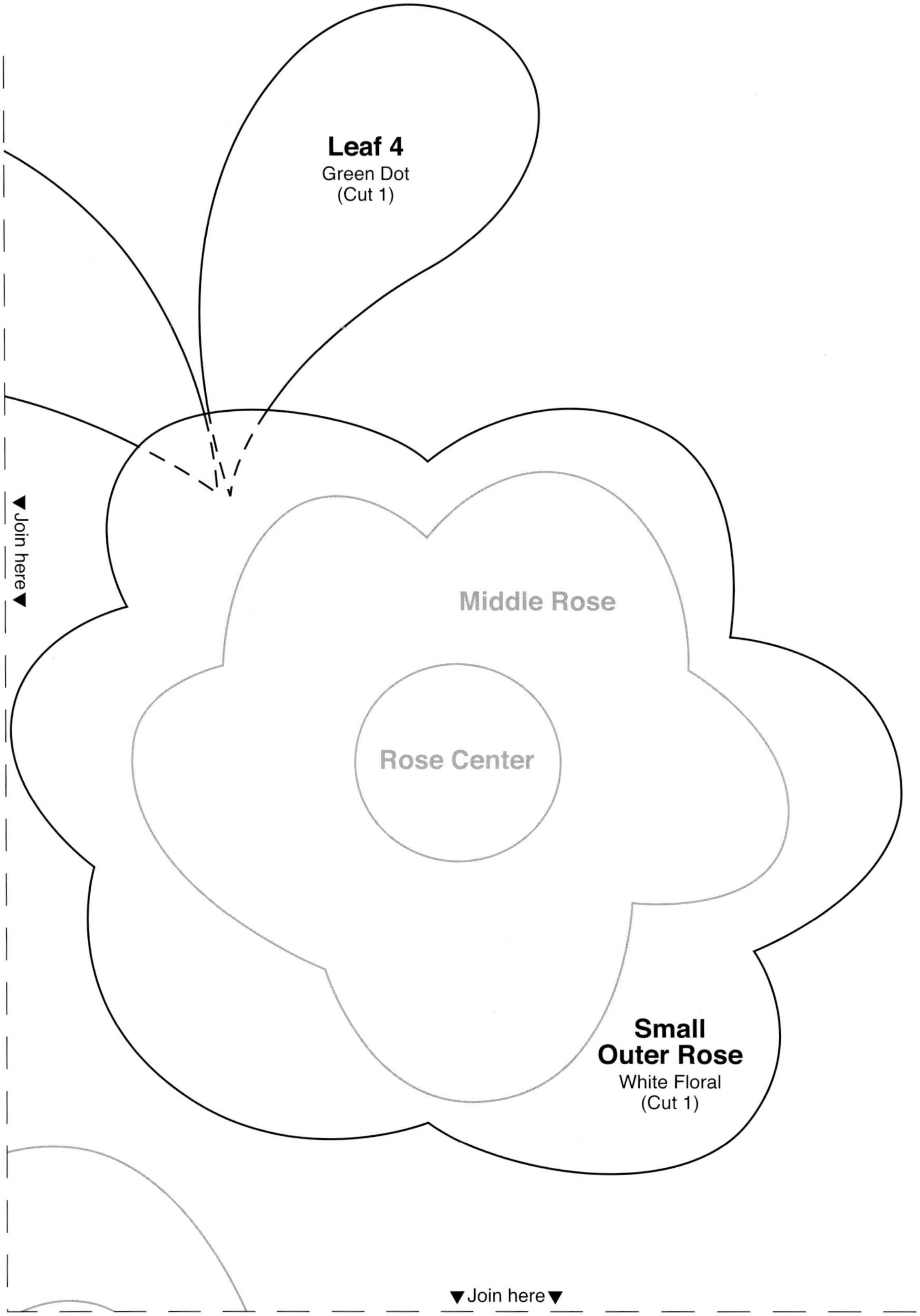

Cabbage Roses Block, cont.

Gardener's Hat Block

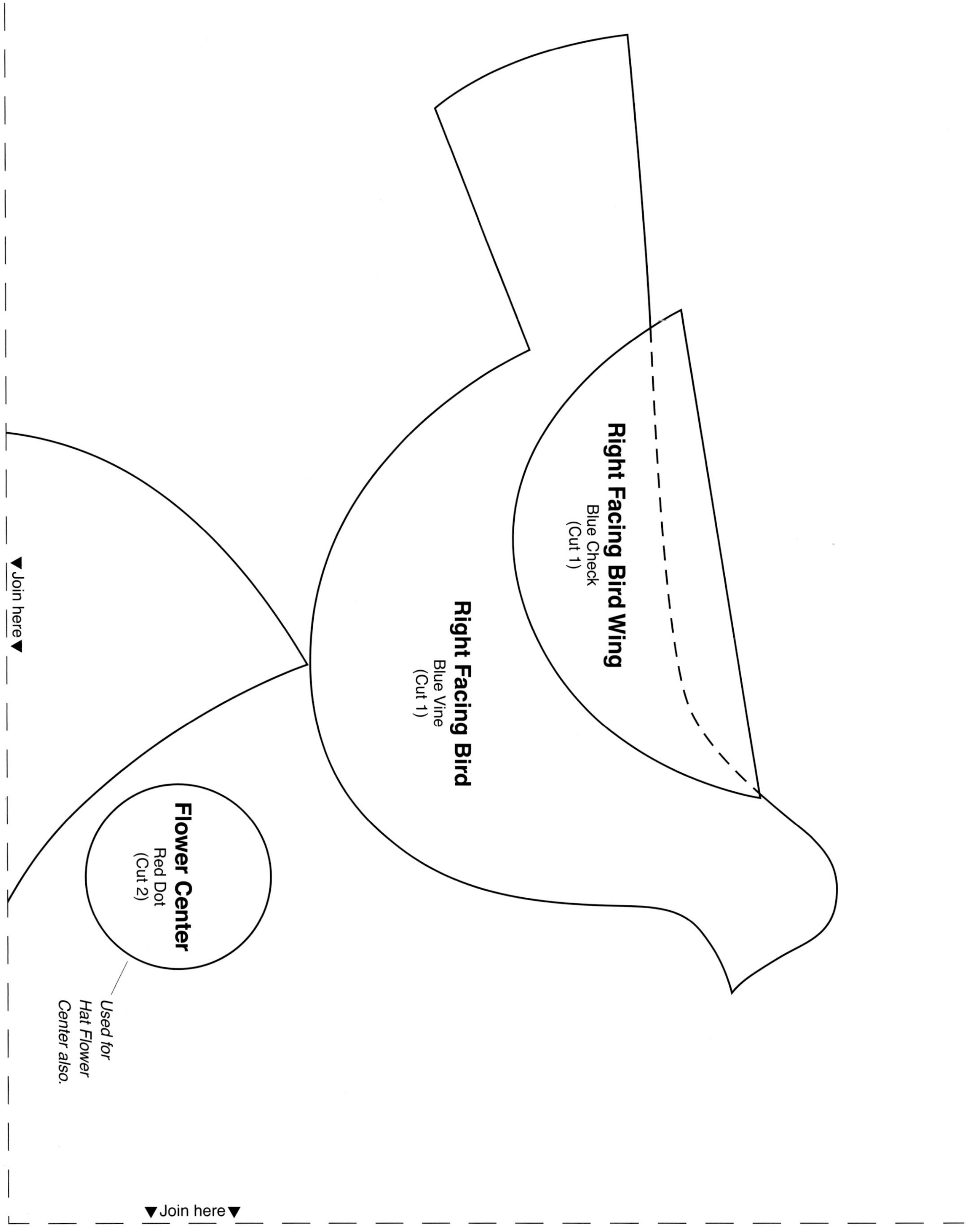

Gardener's Hat Block, cont.

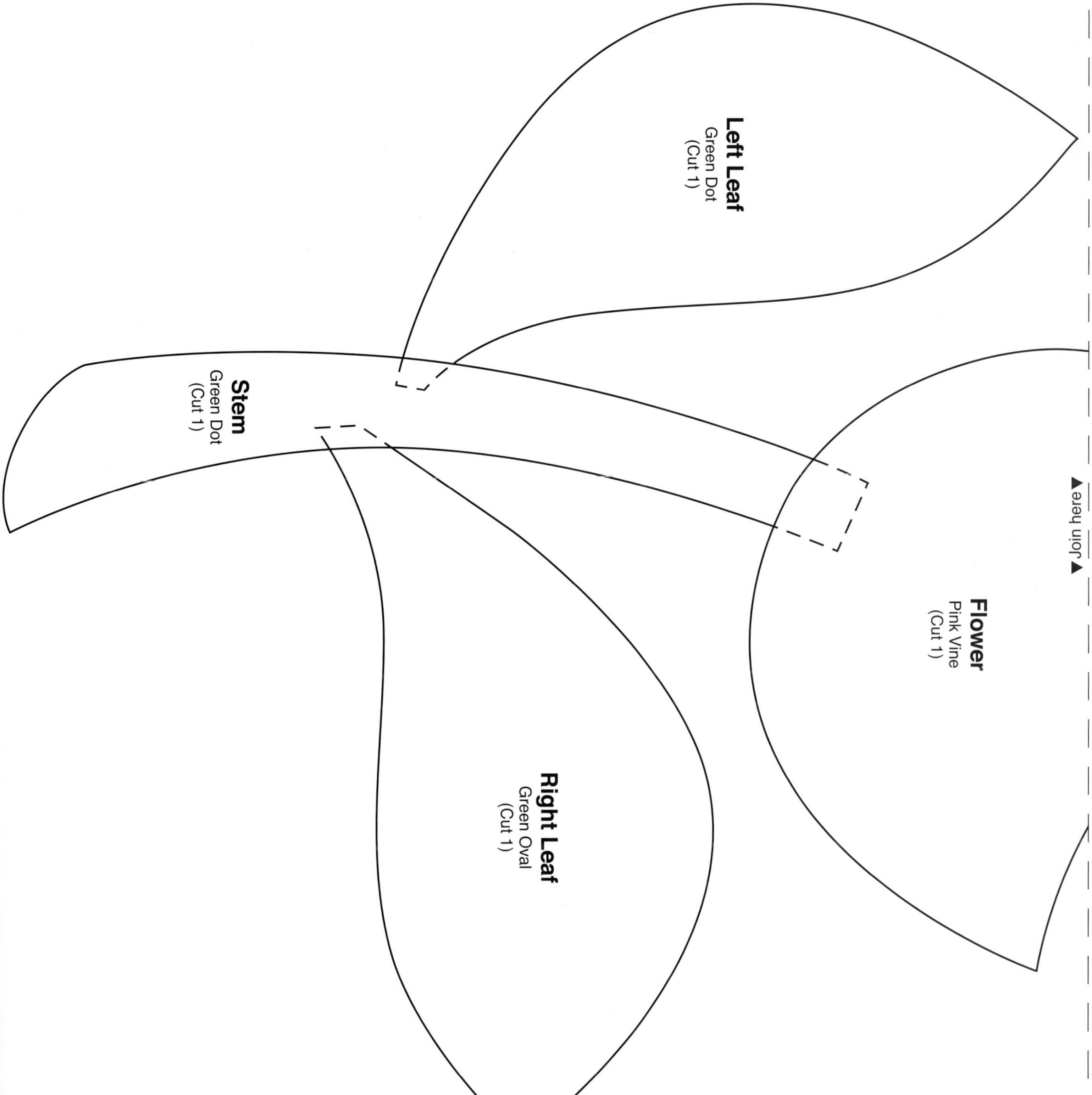

Gardener's Hat Block, cont.

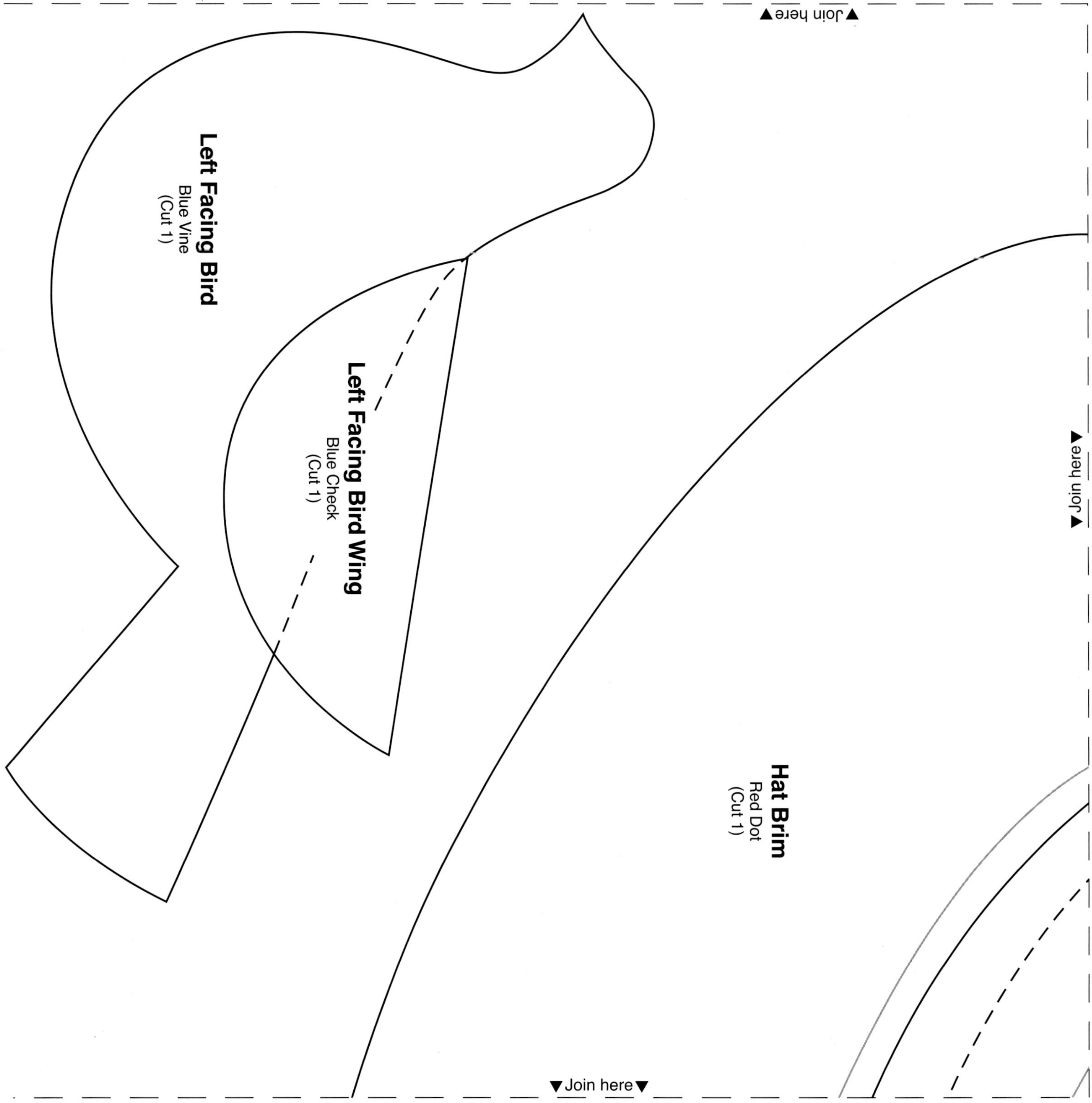

Gardener's Hat Block, cont.

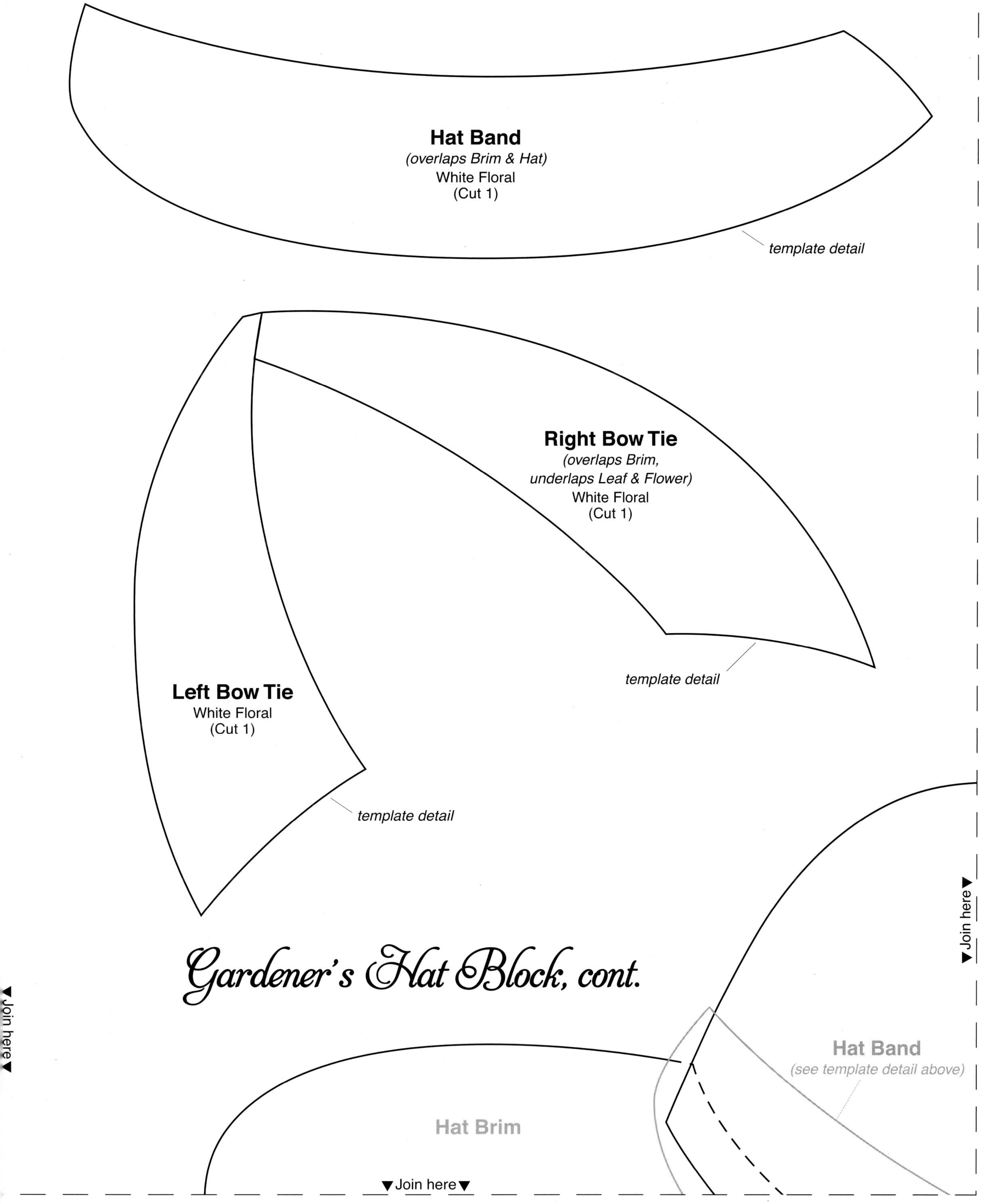

Gardener's Hat Block, cont.

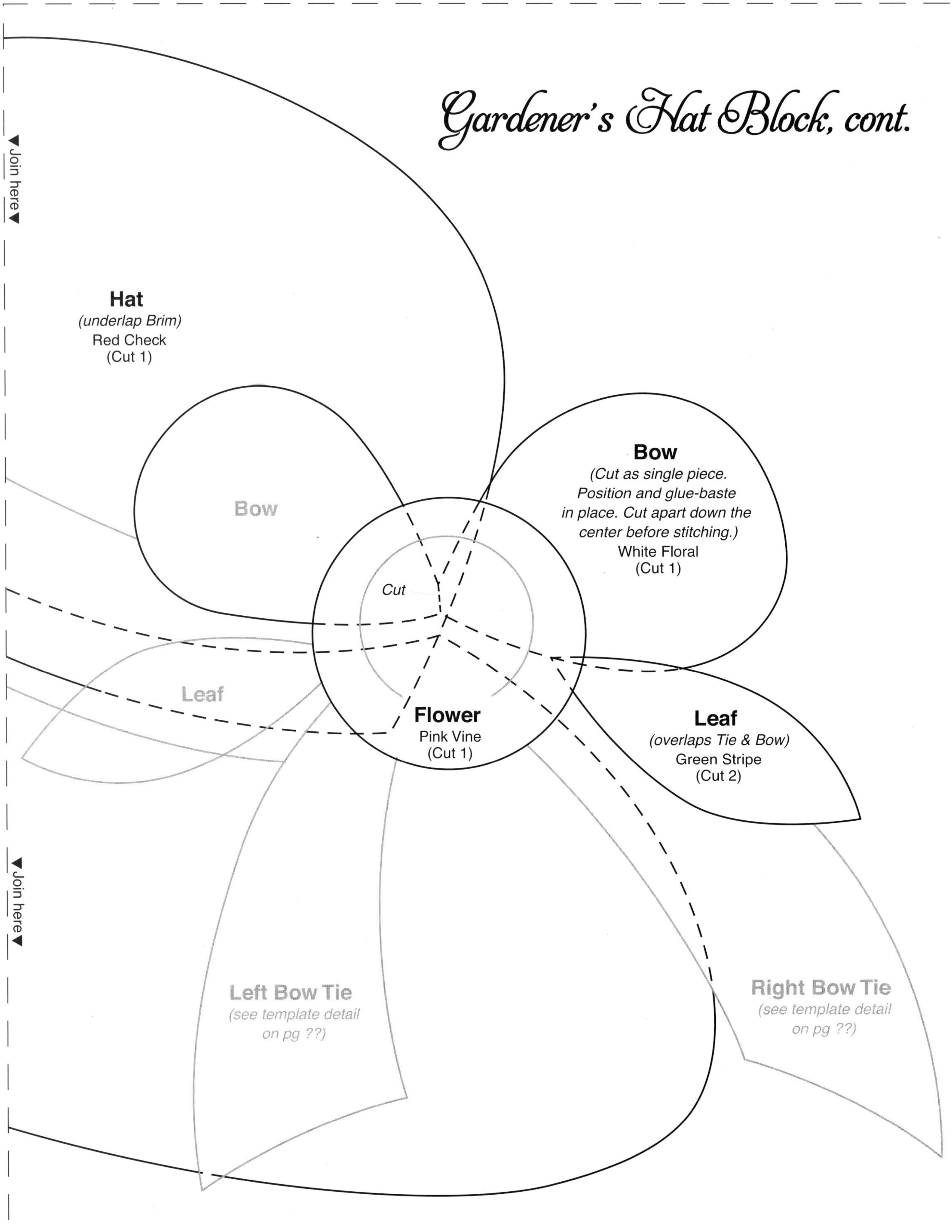

Basket Block

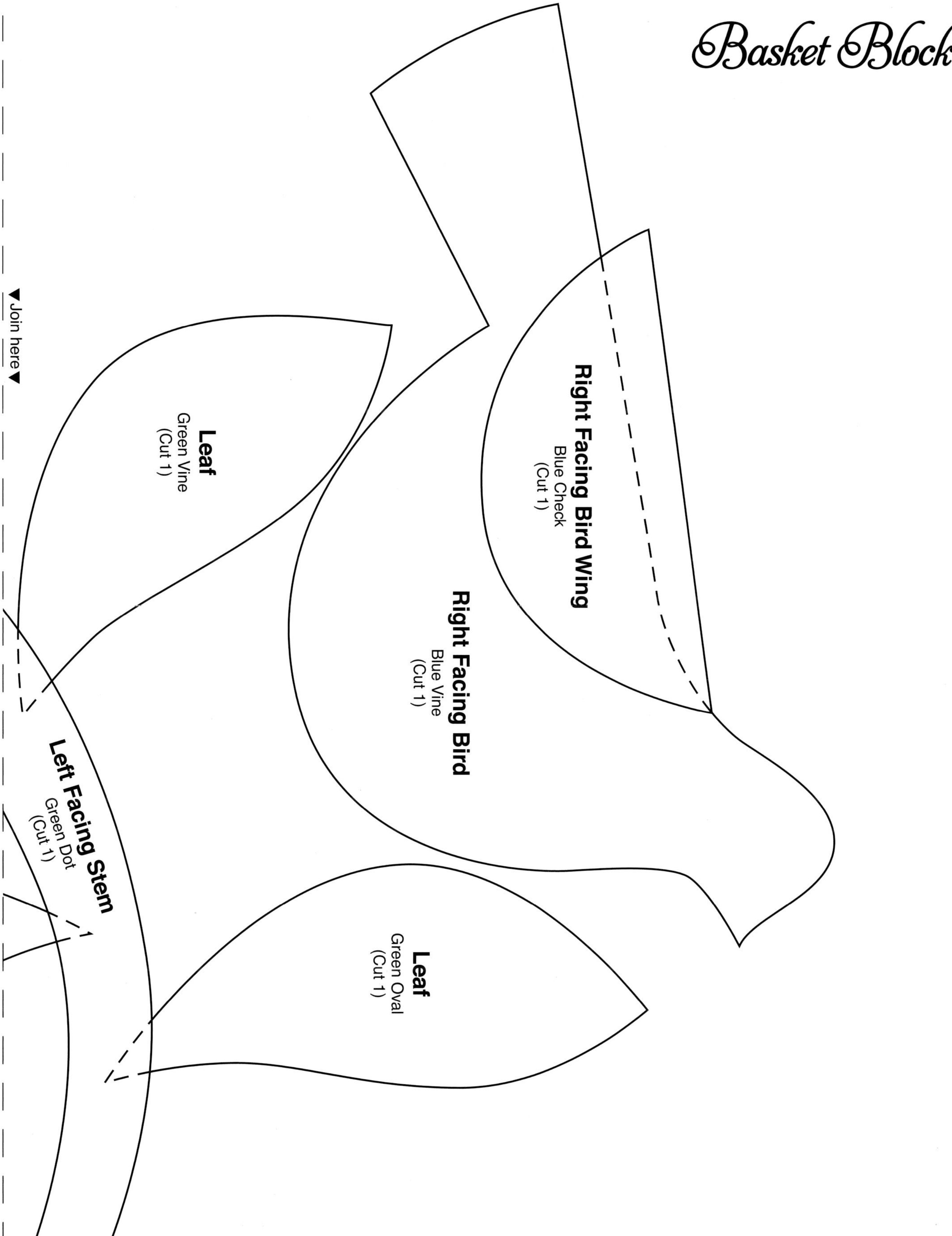

Basket Block, cont.

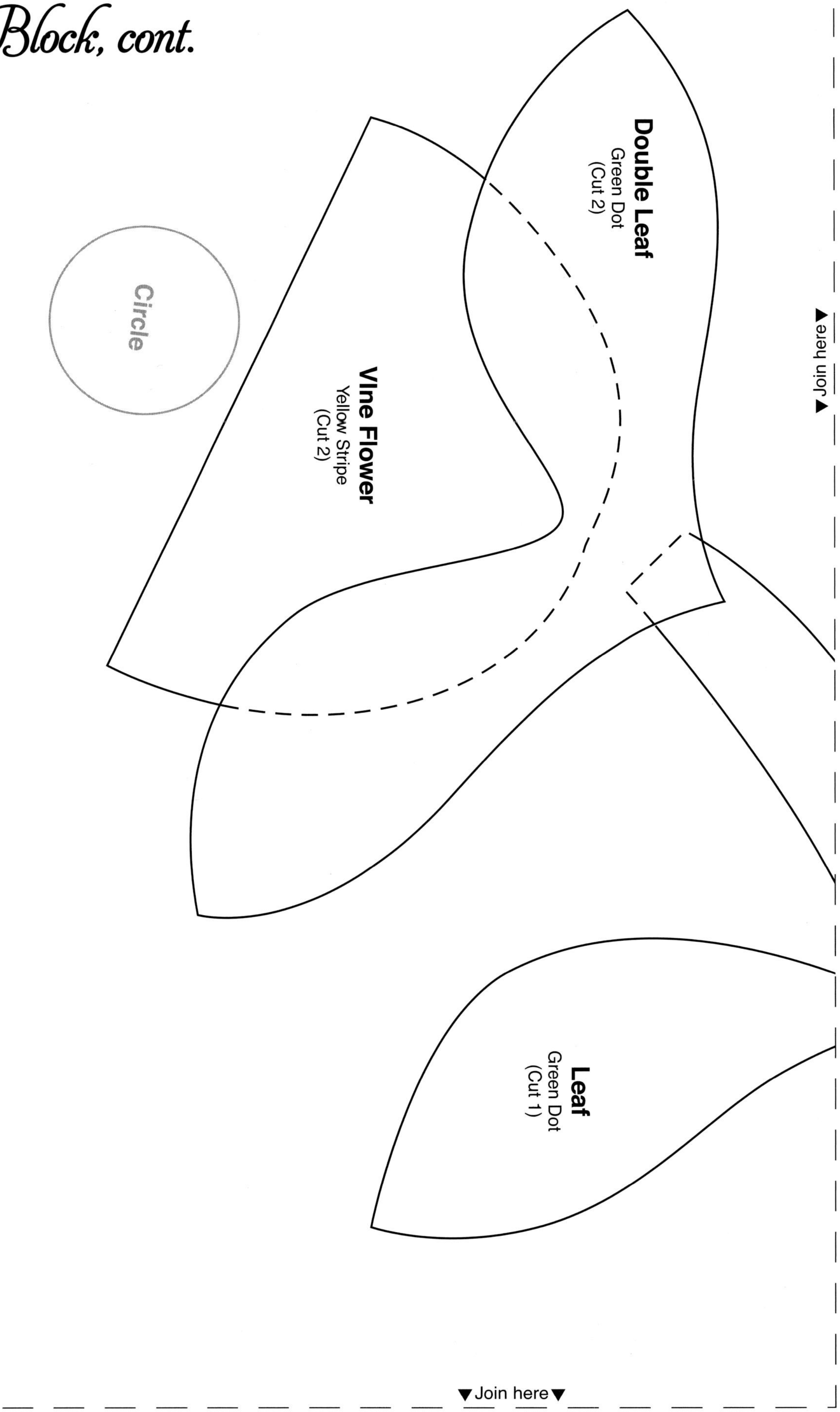

Basket Block, cont.

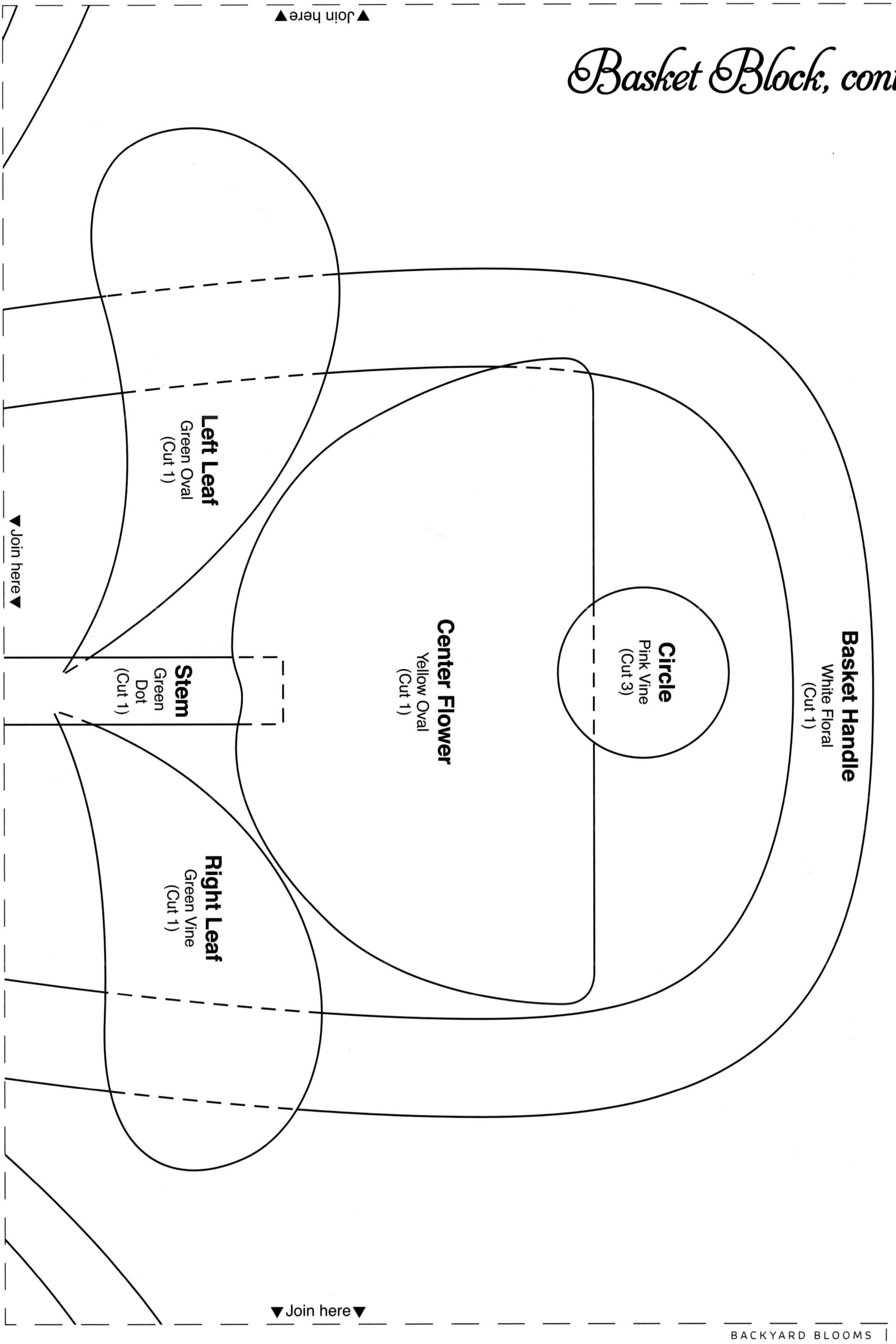

Basket Block, cont.

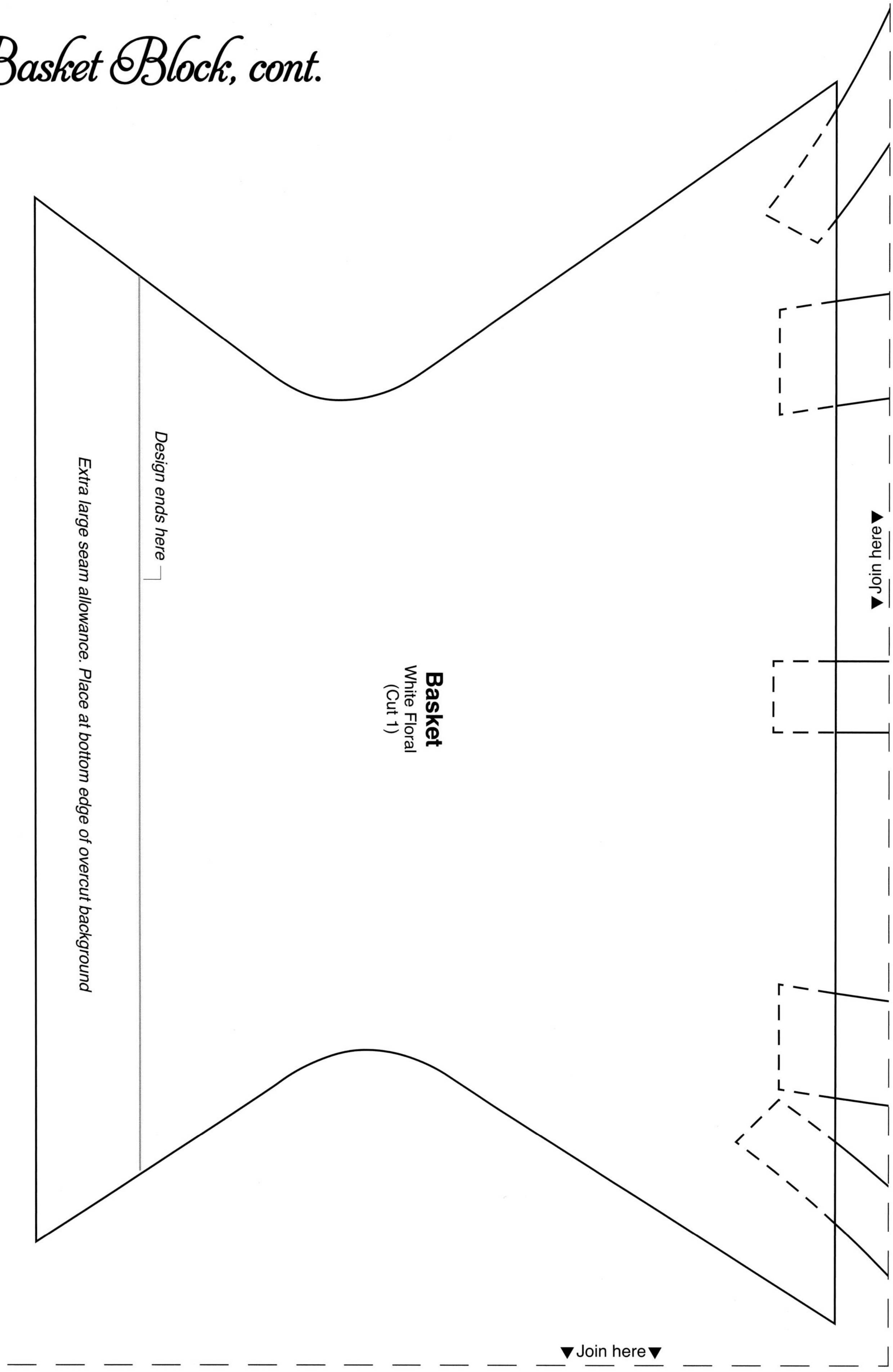

Basket Block, cont.

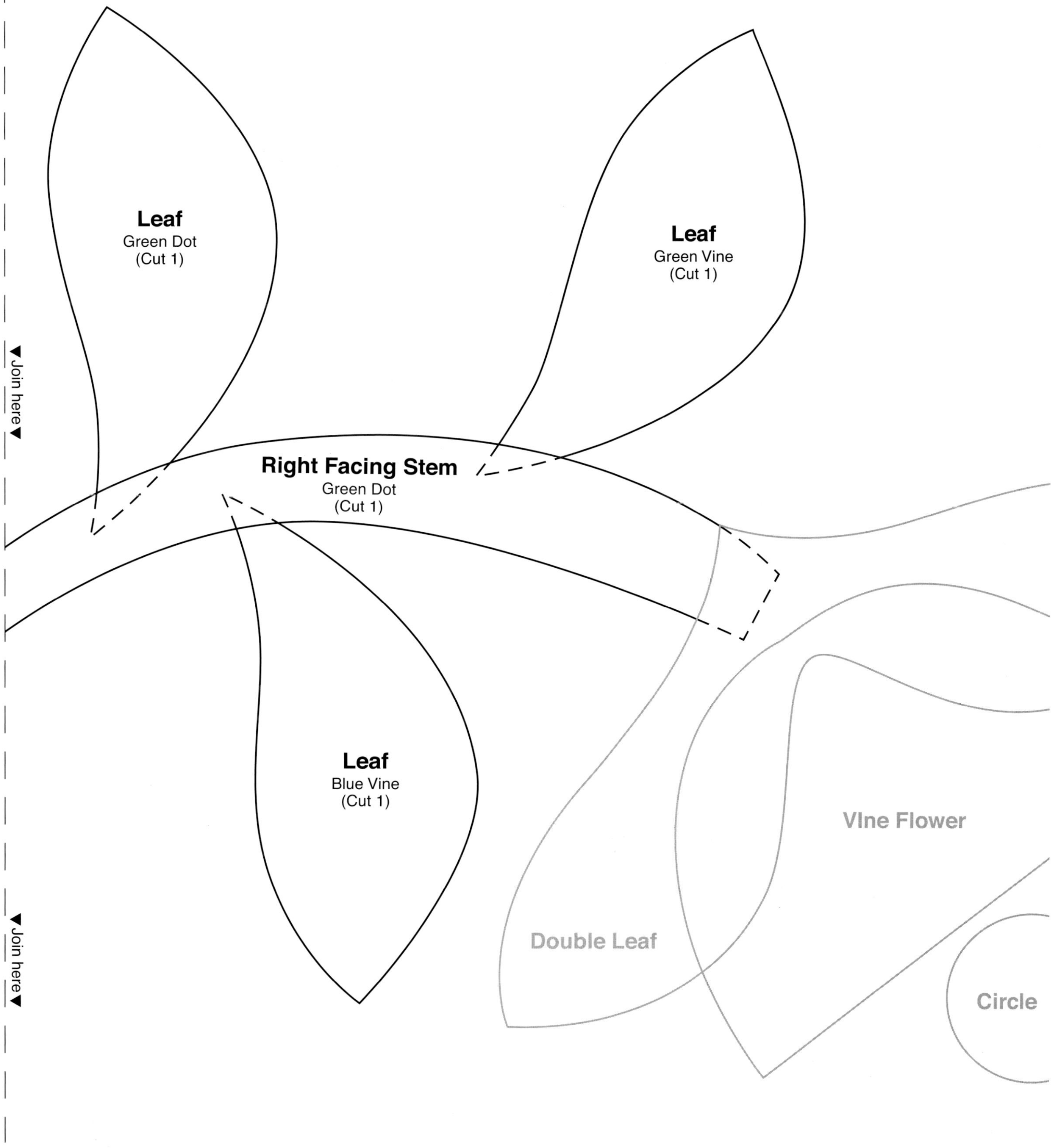

Recipe

Backyard Blooms makes me think of lunch in a garden setting. I particularly like Pecan and Pear Salad and all its variations. Serve with a crusty hot roll and an Arnold Palmer Iced- Tea on the patio or in a garden room!

Pecan and Pear Salad with Gorgonzola

Serves 8

Salad Dressing

1/3 cup raspberry vinegar
1 tsp salt
1/2 cup sugar
1 Tbsp dry mustard
1 1/2 Tbsp minced shallot
3/4 cup salad oil
1 Tbsp poppy seeds

Combine all ingredients well.

Pecan Coating

1 cup pecan halves
2 Tbsp salad oil
1 tsp chili powder (optional)
2 tsp sugar

Preheat oven to 300 degrees. Toss pecans and oil in small bowl. Add chili powder and sugar and toss to coat. Spread on a baking sheet. Bake 10 minutes or until toasted, stirring frequently to avoid burning. Cool.

Roasted Fresh Pears

1 Tbsp butter
1 Tbsp sugar
4 ripe pears

Peel and slice each pear half into 5 pieces. Lay out on a baking sheet and top with butter and sugar. Bake 10 minutes at 500 degrees. Turn over and bake 5 more minutes. Cool.

Salad

Hearts of Romaine Lettuce, torn into bite size pieces
Baby spinach
2 lemons, halved and seeded
Salt and pepper
1/2 cup Gorgonzola crumbles

Toss greens with dressing in a large bowl until well coated. Arrange on individual plates. Sprinkle pecans over greens. Fan pear slices over pecans. Top with gorgonzola crumbles and a grind of pepper. Squeeze a little lemon juice over each serving.

The Anatomical Plates of
Pietro da Cortona

27 Baroque Masterpieces

With a New Introduction by
JEREMY M. NORMAN

DOVER PUBLICATIONS, INC., NEW YORK

Original title-page engraving. TRANSLATIONS: Upper-left cartouche: "The unskilled hand fosters diseases." Upper-right cartouche: "Cures should be effected through science, not through chance." Lower-left statue base: "Transfusion." Lower-right statue base: "The wellspring of the blood." Central band: "To prevent illnesses from destroying the body, it will be helpful to eliminate them."

Published in Canada by General Publishing Company, Ltd., 30 Lesmill Road, Don Mills, Toronto, Ontario.
Published in the United Kingdom by Constable and Company, Ltd., 10 Orange Street, London WC2H 7EG.

This Dover edition, first published in 1986, contains all 27 plates from *Tabulae anatomicae a celeberrimo pictore Petro Berrettino Cortonensi Delineatae, & egregiè aeri incisae nunc primum prodeunt, et a Cajetano Petrioli Romano Doctore, Regis Sardiniae Chirurgo, publico Anatomico, & inter Arcades Erasistrato Coo Notis illustratae. Impensis Fausti Amidei Bibliopolae in via Cursus. Romae, MDCCXLI. Ex Typographia Antonii de Rubeis apud Pantheon in via Seminarii Romani. Superiorum permissu* [Anatomical plates drawn by the very famous painter Pietro Berrettini of Cortona, and excellently engraved on copper, now published for the first time, with explanatory notes by Gaetano Petrioli of Rome, doctor, surgeon to the King of Sardinia, public anatomist and known as Erasistratus Cous in the Academy of the Arcadians. Published by Fausto Amideo, bookseller, via del Corso. Rome, 1741. Printed by Antonio de Rubeis, near the Pantheon, via del Seminario Romano. By permission of the authorities].
The introduction, by Jeremy M. Norman, and the brief identifying captions (based on the original Latin text) are new features, specially prepared for the Dover edition.
The publisher is grateful to Jeremy Norman & Co., Inc., San Francisco, for making this rare first edition available for reproduction.

Manufactured in the United States of America
Dover Publications, Inc., 31 East 2nd Street, Mineola, N.Y. 11501

Library of Congress Cataloging in Publication Data

Pietro, da Cortona, 1596–1669.
The anatomical plates of Pietro da Cortona.

Originally published as: Tabulae anatomicae a celeberrimo pictore Petro Berrettino Cortonensi delineatae. Rome, Fausto Amideo, 1741.
Bibliography: p.
1. Pietro, da Cortona, 1596–1669. 2. Anatomy, Artistic. 3. Drawing, Baroque—Italy. I. Title.
NC257.P46A4 1986 769.92'4 85-29298
ISBN 0-486-25081-4